RISE&
SHINE
&
PRAY

Printed by Createspace.com

First Printing 2018

ISBN 978-1-78808-418-5

Ellerslie Publishing
99 High Park Road ,Ryde,
Isle of Wight PO33 1BZ UK

HOW TO USE THIS PRAYER JOURNAL

When I came across prayer journaling, I was over 45 years and have been a Christian for over 25 years, so I was late to the party! But now I have discovered it, I love it for the following reasons:

❖ Prayer always draws us closer to God

❖ Tracking prayer requests by writing them down serves as a reminder to actually pray.

❖ Writing down prayer needs serves as a reinforcement to remember the individual needs.

❖ Keeping a prayer journal encourages us to have a place to record praises!

❖ Writing out prayers encourages our minds to purposely choose our words and allows our hearts to engage in meaningful conversations God gave me the gift of art and I wanted to use it while I prayed.

When you use this journal, feel free to sketch, draw, stick pictures, photos, fabric (whatever takes your fancy) to this book. I have written verses but I suggest you look them up and copy them in your own writing. This will help you to learn the bible verses and reflect on what they mean to you.

YOURS IN CHRIST,

Bev Jessup

NAMES OF GOD

There are lots of different names of God in the bible. Spend time thinking how you could illustrate the following:

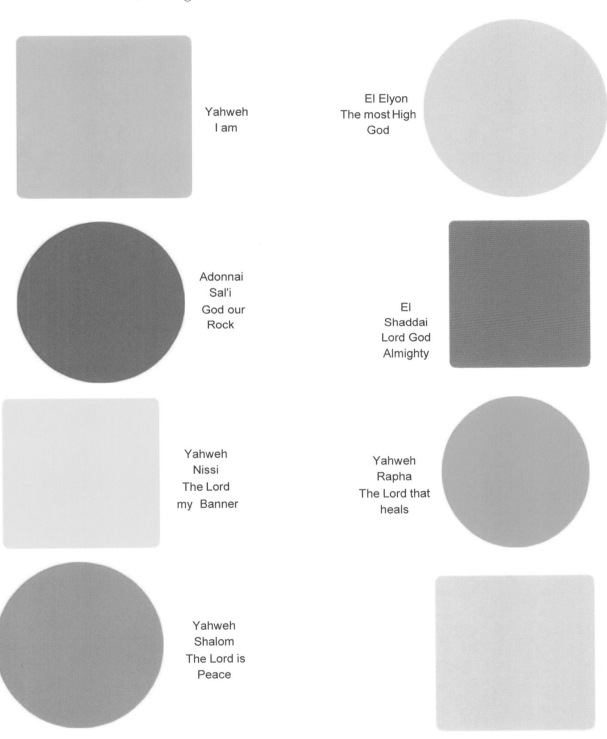

Yahweh
I am

El Elyon
The most High
God

Adonnai
Sal'i
God our
Rock

El
Shaddai
Lord God
Almighty

Yahweh
Nissi
The Lord
my Banner

Yahweh
Rapha
The Lord that
heals

Yahweh
Shalom
The Lord is
Peace

There are lots of different names of God in the bible. Spend time thinking how you could illustrate the following:

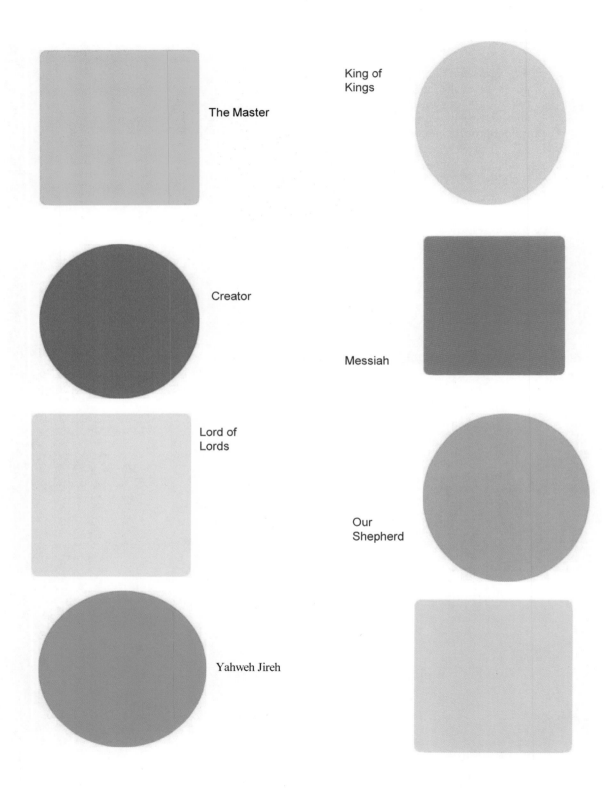

The Master

King of Kings

Creator

Messiah

Lord of Lords

Our Shepherd

Yahweh Jireh

The Lord's Prayer

OUR FATHER IN HEAVEN HALLOWED BE YOUR NAME

Consider your Father in Heaven and find these verses,
write them down in the space provided and pray.

1 Chronicles 29: 10-13

Psalm 135: 13

Psalm 113:1-3

Your
Kingdom come
Your will be done
on earth as in
heaven.

Consider His Kingdom and find these verses, write them down in the space provided and pray.

2 Chronicles 7 :14

Philippians 2 :9-11

Isaiah 59:19

Give us Today

Our Daily Bread

Consider His Provision and Word and find these verses, write them down in the space provided (use different colours) and pray.

Psalm 73:28

Matthew 6:8

Matthew 6:26

Matthew 6:33

James 1:17

Psalm 37:23-24

Psalm 55:22

Psalm 37:4 - 5

Forgive us Our Sins

Stick an envelope here with the flap facing
you and write on the cover
SINS TAKEN BY CHRIST

You can write your sins here and stick
them in the envelope

As we Forgive those
who
Sin against us

Consider your sins, find these verses, write them down in the space provided (use different colours) and pray.

James 4:9

James 4:8

John 3:30

Psalm 139:23-24

Psalm 51

Romans 8:1-2

LEAD US NOT INTO TEMPTATION

BUT DELIVER US FROM EVIL

Consider your temptations, find these verses, write them down in the space provided (use different colours) and pray.

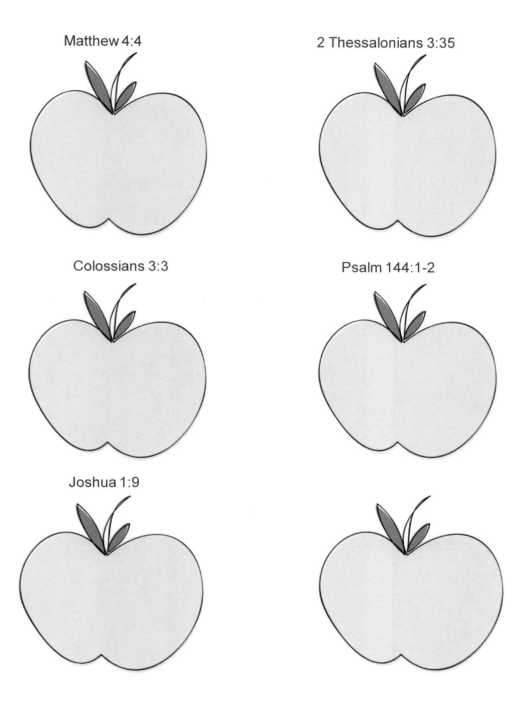

Matthew 4:4

2 Thessalonians 3:35

Colossians 3:3

Psalm 144:1-2

Joshua 1:9

For your kingdom come, the
power and the glory are
yours forever and ever.

Consider His Majesty & Power, find these verses, write them down in the space provided (use different colours) and pray.

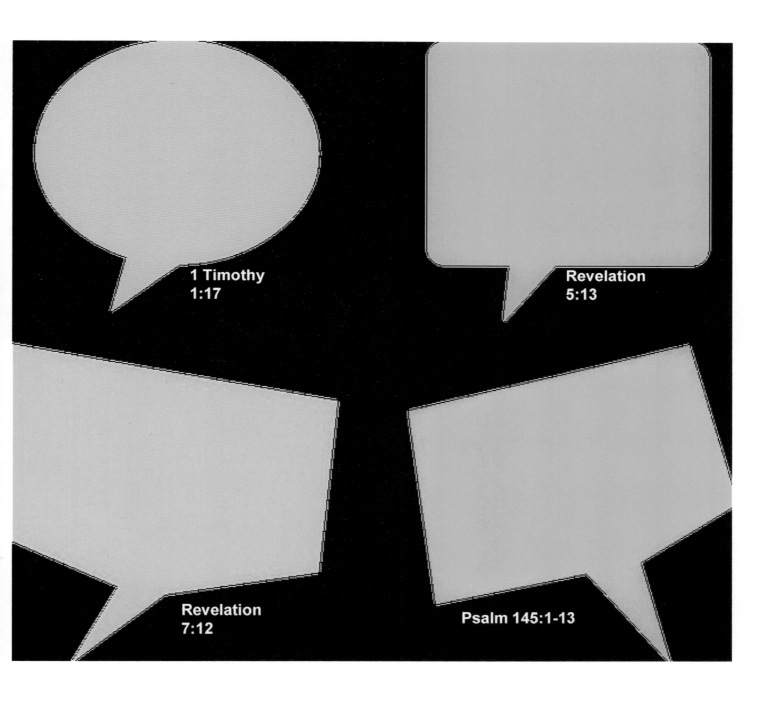

Praise Letters to God

You have a few blank pages to write letters to God about the things you want to thank him for and draw pictures of those things to brighten up your page. I have even written words to praise songs, so I can sing them to God.

DAILY PRAYERS

When friends and family ask for prayer, commit their
petition to a day and then you will not forget!

MONDAY

TUESDAY

WEDNESDAY

THURSDAY

FRIDAY

SATURDAY

SUNDAY

MY FAMILY

Thank you God for all
the blessings to me
and my family. For the
Strength you give me
and for all the people
around me who
make my life
meaningful

In the next few pages, you will have a picture frame in which you can insert a photo or draw your own picture of your loved one in your family.

Write their name at the top of each page and consider what you would pray about for each one.

PRAYER IDEAS

* work * relationships * school * university * future spouses * relationship with God * Friends * Guidance * church

----

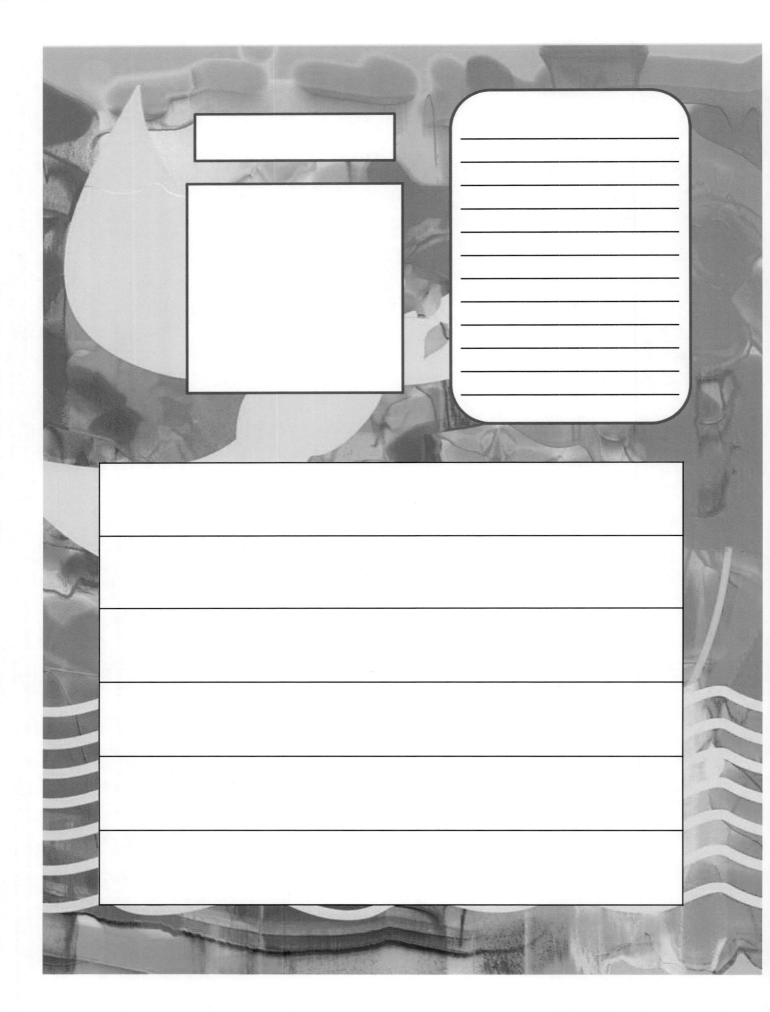

Challenges

ROMANS 8;1 - 2

So now there is no condemnation for those who belong to Christ Jesus and because you belong to him, the power of the life - giving Spirit has freed you from the power of sn that leads to death.

Jesus tells us that we will have troubles in this world, it's a guarantee. However, He also promises that we have victory through our faith because Jesus Christ has overcome the world. If you are facing hard and uncertain times, you can be encouraged to press on knowing that you are an over-comer! Write your challenges on the stones below and pray for His strength.

Be strong and courageous. Do not be afraid or terrified because of them, for the LORD your God goes with you; he will never leave you nor forsake you.

DEUT 31;6

Often we think because our trial is big to us, that it will be too big for God Almighty. But God is able to handle anything we go through, and He does that for every person who calls on Him. Write your challenges on the stones below and pray for His strength.

So do not fear, for I am with you;
do not be dismayed, for I am your
God. I will strengthen you and
help you; I will uphold you with
my righteous right hand.

ISAIAH 41;10

When we are in a trial, it seems like it will never end, But God is a God of all time; He knows exactly how long our trials will endure and He will give us the strength we need to get through them. Write your challenges on the stones below and pray for His strength.

"Trust in the Lord with all your heart and do not lean on your own understanding. In all your ways acknowledge him, and he will make your paths straight."

(Proverbs 3:5-6)

Trials have a way of wearing us down and before long, we don't think we can put one weary foot in front of another. The enemy of our soul whispers that we are alone and that we will never make it. God reassures us that He is with us. God will give us the strength we need; He will help us and will uphold us. And if God upholds us, we're going to be okay.

"But the Helper, the Holy Spirit, whom the Father will send in my name, he will teach you all things and bring to your remembrance all that I have said to you.

John 14:26

CREATIVE PRAYER PAINTINGS

Now is your opportunity to draw,
colour and paint your own creations
and pray while you do so.

Colour & Pray

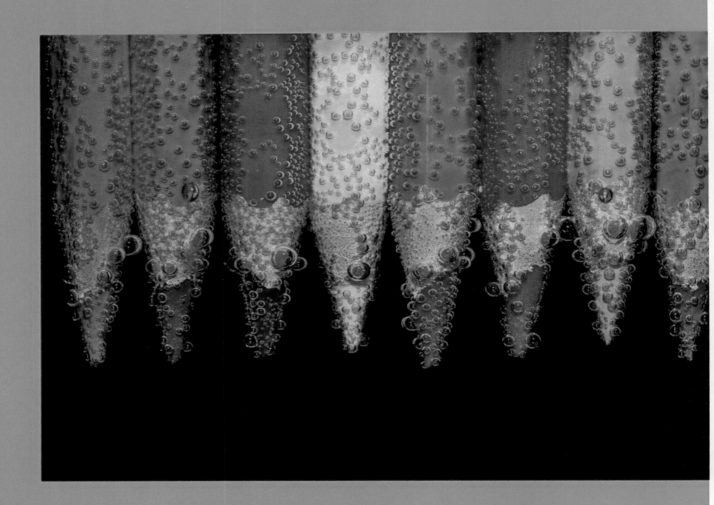

You might like to colour and pray

Cloud Prayers

Sometimes we only seem to have time for quick prayers that we do not want to forget. Jot down key prayer points in each cloud

Dear God

Sometimes we have a lot to say
to God and it helps to write it in
a letter form as if you are writing
to your best friend.
After all, Jesus wants to have a
relationship with you and he is
the 'bestest' friend you could
ever have in the world.

Consider His Majesty
them down in the space
and pray.

Prayer Quotes

The next few pages allows you to
collect and reflect on quotes said by
influential or just ordinary people in
your life about prayer. Hopefully they
will encourage you to take prayer
seriously when you are going
through a dry patch, which we all
experience from time to time.

When you can't
put your prayers
into words,
God
hears
your
heart.

Don't pray when you feel like it. Have an appointment with the Lord and keep it. A man is more powerful on his knees.

CORRIE TEN BOOM

To be a Christian without prayer is no more possible than to be alive without breathing.

MARTIN LUTHER

God speaks in the silence of the heart. Listening is the beginning of prayer.

MOTHER THERESA

ARMOUR OF GOD

" Finally, be strong in the Lord and in his mighty power. Put on the full armour of God so that you can take your stand against the devil's schemes. For our struggle is not against flesh and blood, but against the rulers, against the authorities, against the powers of this dark world and against the spiritual forces of evil in the heavenly realms. Therefore, put on the full armour of God, so that when the day of evil comes, you may be able to stand your ground, and after you have done everything to stand, stand firm then, with the belt of truth buckled around your waist, with the breast plate of righteousness in place, and with your feet fitted with the readiness that comes from the gospel of peace. In addition to all this, take up the shield of faith, with which you can extinguish all the flaming arrows of the evil one. Take the helmet of salvation and sword of the Spirit which is the word of God. And pray in the spirit on all occasions, with all kinds of prayers and requests. With this in mind, be alert and always keep on praying for all the saints."

Ephesians. 6:10-18

Over the next few pages, mentally pray through each part of the armour and reflect on the verses chosen on each page. Write them out and commit them to your mind in your time of prayer.

The belt of truth is the first part of the armour listed because, without truth, we are lost, and the schemes of the devil will surely overpower us.

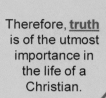

Therefore, **truth** is of the utmost importance in the life of a Christian.

BELT OF TRUTH

JOHN 17;17

JOHN 14;6

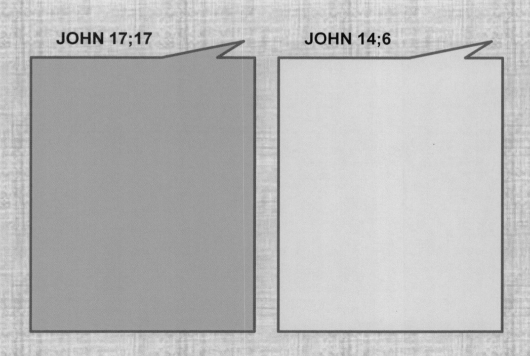

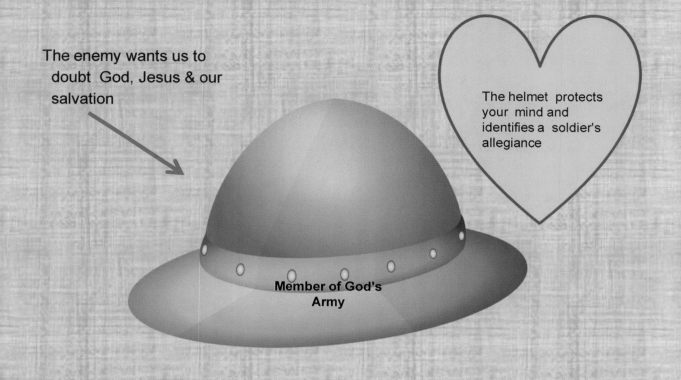

The enemy wants us to doubt God, Jesus & our salvation

The helmet protects your mind and identifies a soldier's allegiance

Member of God's Army

HELMET OF SALVATION

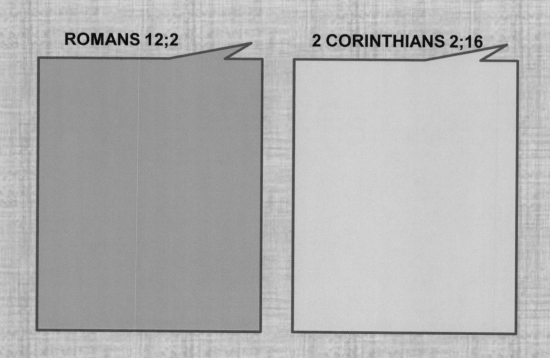

ROMANS 12;2

2 CORINTHIANS 2;16

Satan attacks our hearts, emotions, self-worth and trust. He accuses us of being guilty and unworthy

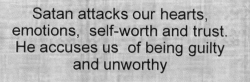

Guards our hearts against the accusations and charges of Satan and secures our innermost being from his attacks

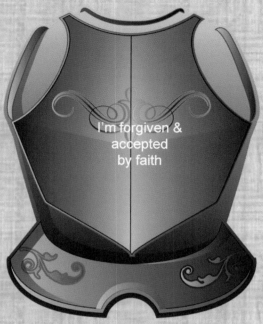

I'm forgiven & accepted by faith

BREAST PLATE OF RIGHTEOUSNESS

1 JOHN 1;9

ISAIAH 61;10

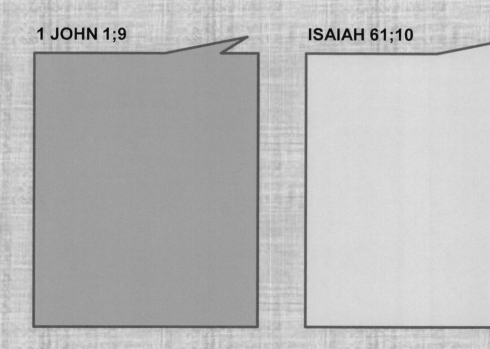

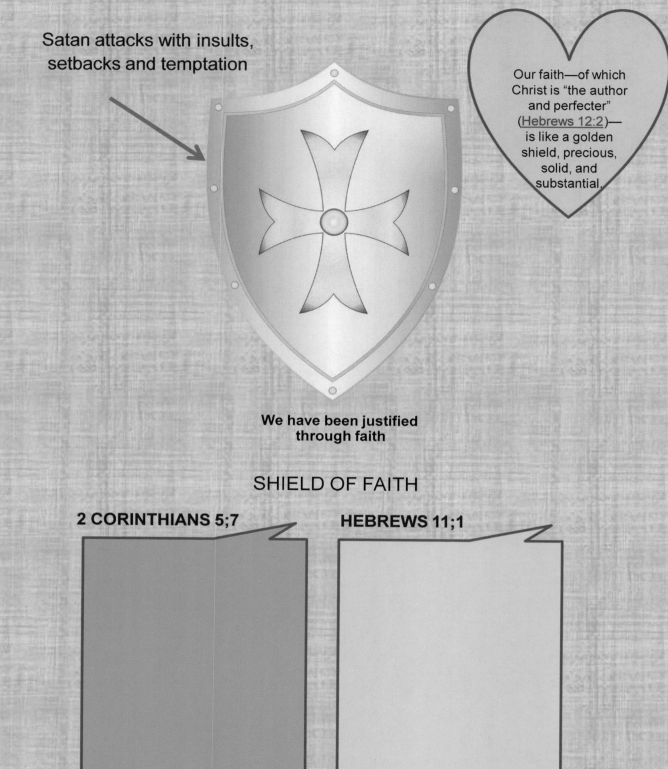

Satan attacks with insults, setbacks and temptation

Our faith—of which Christ is "the author and perfecter" (Hebrews 12:2)— is like a golden shield, precious, solid, and substantial.

We have been justified through faith

SHIELD OF FAITH

2 CORINTHIANS 5;7

HEBREWS 11;1

The sword of the Spirit works.
Memorize Scripture and use
the Word of God to defeat

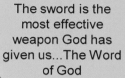

The sword is the
most effective
weapon God has
given us...The Word
of God

SWORD OF THE SPIRIT

JOHN 1;1

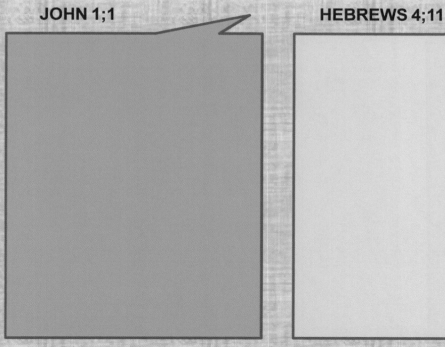

HEBREWS 4;11

When Satan comes against your tranquility, he throws out stones and briars of doubts and discouragement to cause you to stumble.

The shoes also allows us to be ready to spread the Good News and to have a firm footing.

SHOES OF PEACE

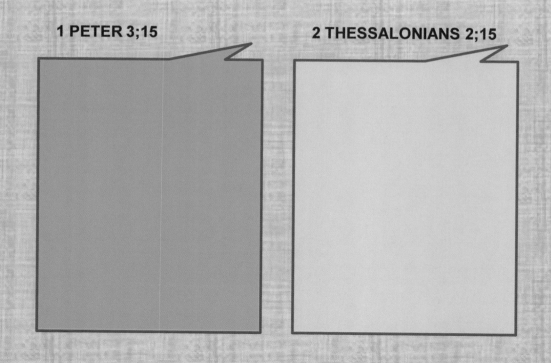

1 PETER 3;15

2 THESSALONIANS 2;15

The Prayer Art Journal combines two joys in one; focus on prayer while relaxing in Art and one's own creativity. This guided journal helps you enjoy your time with God and still personalise the pages with your own writing of bible verses and drawings.

Made in the USA
Columbia, SC
18 April 2018